FREE TIME ACTIVITIES

FOR AGES
5-7

MOLLY POTTER

A & C BLACK

Colossal thanks to...

Anna Sims for coping so well with my regular bouts of over excitement.

Published 2008 by A & C Black Publishers Ltd
38 Soho Square, London W1D 3HB
www.acblack.com

ISBN 978-0-7136-8976-1

Written by Molly Potter
Design by Cathy Tincknell
Illustration by Mike Phillips

Copyright © Molly Potter 2008

Printed in Great Britain by Martins the Printers, Berwick-on- Tweed

This book is produced using paper that is made from wood grown in managed, sustainable forests. It is natural, renewable and recyclable. The logging and manufacturing processes conform to the environmental regulations of the country of origin.

To see our full range of books visit
www.acblack.com

CONTENTS

INTRODUCTION

WHY WOULD YOU USE THIS BOOK?

It can be exhausting perpetually inventing new ideas to keep children purposefully and happily occupied – a task many teachers, club leaders and teaching assistants are faced with every day. *Free Time Activities* provides ready-made, interesting, varied and quirky ideas that can be used with individuals or groups of children in many different settings e.g.

• Breakfast clubs
• After school clubs
• Any children's club
• Last minute cover for a class or group of children
• For end of term fun
• During wet breaks
• As golden time or a treat for an individual pupil or group of pupils

Each activity has clear instructions and those designed for individual work require minimal teacher intervention.Children will be inspired and entertained by the activities in this book and motivation to do them should not be an issue. Most of the activities require little more than a pencil and a vivid imagination!

> *Imagination is more important than knowledge...*
> ALBERT EINSTEIN US (GERMAN-BORN) PHYSICIST (1879 - 1955)

HOW IS THE BOOK ORGANISED?

The activities in this book are split into three sections.
Section 1: Activities best completed by individual children
Section 2: Activities suited to pairs or small groups of children
Section 3: Activities for a group of children, ideally led by an adult

Equipment is deliberately kept to a minimum and a list of what's needed for each activity is provided on the contents page. Most of the activities in the first two sections simply require a photocopy of the activity and then a pencil, coloured pens and, in some instances, extra paper. The activities that are led by an adult (in the third section) for the most part can be done by reading directly from the book, although sometimes a photocopy of the page is essential to help pupils complete the task. With these particular activities we recommend that the supervising adult selects an activity and prepares any equipment that might be needed in advance.

HOW COULD THE ACTIVITIES BE EXTENDED AND PRESENTED?

Most of the ideas could be extended in one way or another and need not end with the task that is laid out on the page. On some pages there are specific suggestions listed under 'More to do!' but here are some generic examples of how this can be done, although not all of these examples will be suitable for all activities.

CHILDREN COULD:

- Make their own version of the activity, or they could alter or add some ideas to the existing one.
- Devise their own extension activity, present it to the class or group, and then vote on the one they would all like to do.
- Explain to another child what they did – perhaps without using words!
- Add to or colour in any picture or turn it into a collage.
- Give each other positive feedback on how well the task was completed.
- Work out a way of evaluating or ranking the activities for enjoyment, difficulty, humour, etc.
- Vote for any activity or part of an activity they might like to do or see again (particularly relevant to drama activities).
- Produce a letter, postcard, interview, advert, radio advert, newspaper report, poster, quiz, memory test, puzzle, fact bubbles, time-line, labelled diagrams, questionnaire, list, map, cartoon, graph to do with the activity.

YOU COULD:

- Make a display of any ideas that were produced from the activities.
- Create a book of the ideas, pictures or materials the children have produced.
- Photograph or video some of the activities for a classroom display or to show to other classes or assemblies.
- Use one of the activities, especially the drama ones, as the focus for a class assembly.

GUESS DESIGN COPY
DRAW IMAGINE
CONSIDER MAKE UP ACT CUT
EXPLAIN DISCUSS BALANCE, ADJUST
LAUGH DEVELOP
PRETEND PICTURE THINK
QUESTION
MIME, SORT WONDER
COLOUR PLAN DESCRIBE
IMPROVE PONDER ILLUSTRATE
INVENT

Free Time Activities 5-7 © Molly Potter 2008

MUDDLE HEADS

Bob, Tim, Ted and Zug have got themselves into a bit of a muddle. Sort them out by drawing them again but this time with the right bits!

Bob

Ted

Tim

Zug

- Bob and Zug need to swap ears. • Ted and Zug need to swap mouths. •
- Ted and Tim need to swap noses. • Zug and Tim need to swap hair. •
- Tim and Bob need to swap eyes. •

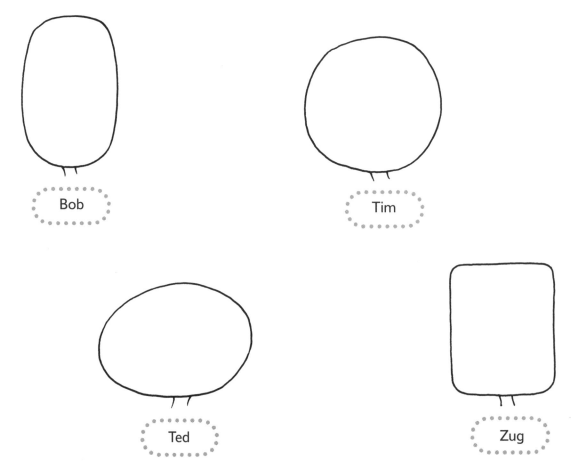

Bob

Tim

Ted

Zug

Answer on p63

LETTER HUNT

Begin at the start and follow the clues that will tell you how to find some letters. Keep the letters in the order that you pick them up. Once you have all the letters, they will spell a word.

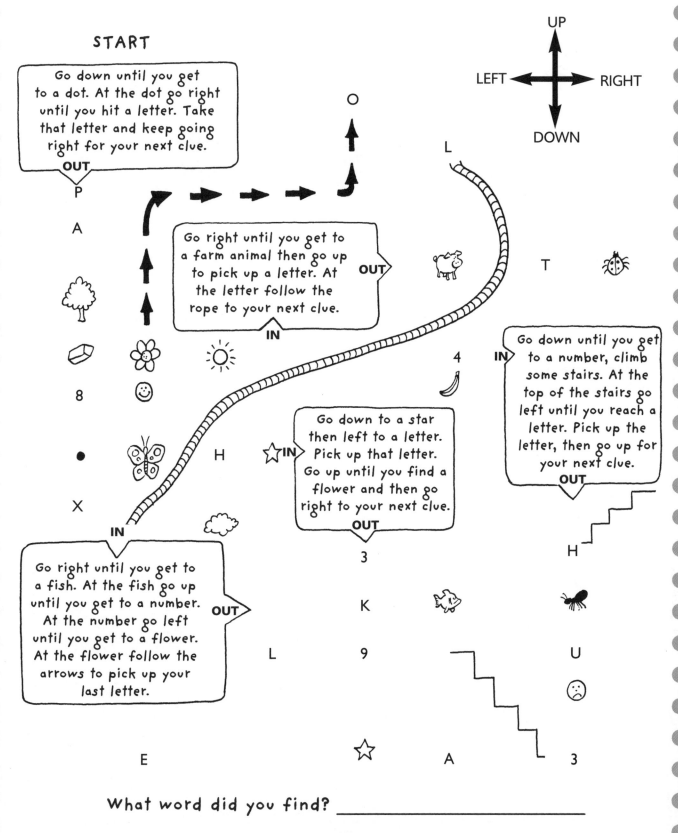

START

Go down until you get to a dot. At the dot go right until you hit a letter. Take that letter and keep going right for your next clue.
OUT

UP

LEFT ← → RIGHT

DOWN

Go right until you get to a farm animal then go up to pick up a letter. At the letter follow the rope to your next clue.
OUT
IN

Go down until you get to a number, climb some stairs. At the top of the stairs go left until you reach a letter. Pick up the letter, then go up for your next clue.
OUT

Go down to a star then left to a letter. Pick up that letter. Go up until you find a flower and then go right to your next clue.
OUT

IN

Go right until you get to a fish. At the fish go up until you get to a number. At the number go left until you get to a flower. At the flower follow the arrows to pick up your last letter.
OUT

What word did you find? _____

Answer on p63

Free Time Activities 5-7 © Molly Potter 2008

SPOT WHAT'S THE SAME

Lag and Yip are best friends and often copy each other.
Ring all the things they have that are the same.
How many can you find?

LAG   ZIP

Now you try and draw two different creatures. They could be people,
monsters, animals or aliens. Include at least ten things that are the
same in both pictures.

Free Time Activities 5-7 © Molly Potter 2008

Answer on p63

CHOSEN NAME

Nine children all gave themselves a new name from this list.

Karinta	Tilempapa	Toplix
Solly	Fanaf	Punnip
Soomp	Prush	Flinta

From what the children said, can you work out which name each child chose?
Start with the names you can be sure about. Nobody chose the same name!

.... A REMINDER ....
A syllable is the number of sound parts a word has.
Cow has 1 syllable, donkey has 2 syllables, elephant has 3 syllables and
alligator has 4.

My name has just 1 syllable.
I hate the letter 'o'.

Name: _____

My name starts with a
different letter from everyone
else'.
Name: _____

My name has only 1 syllable.

Name: _____

My name has 6 letters.

Name: _____

My name begins and ends
with the same letter.

Name: _____

My name is spelt the same
forwards and backwards.

Name: _____

My name has 4 syllables.

Name: _____

I don't like the letter 'p'. My
name has an 'a' in it.

Name: _____

My name has 5 letters.

Name: _____

MORE TO DO!
Can you work out another name that each of the children might like?

Answer on p63

Free Time Activities 5-7 © Molly Potter 2008

SCRUFFY SERENA

This is Scruffy Serena and her pet dog Scruff. She needs to be made to look smart. Give her a complete makeover and draw her looking smart.

SCRUFFY SERENA   SMART SERENA

Free Time Activities 5-7 © Molly Potter 2008

MY WONDERFUL GARDEN

Write a number in each gap and then draw the garden
you have created.

In my garden there are ___ small blue trees and ___ larger
orange trees.

In each of the blue trees, you can see ___ purple plums growing.

In the garden there are __ large red flowers. Each red flower has
__ petals.

There are also ___ smaller pink flowers.

In my garden you can always see __ green and yellow birds flying
around.

In my garden there are always ___ colourful snails crawling around
in the grass.

Add some insects to your garden.

Free Time Activities 5-7 © Molly Potter 2008

HOLIDAY SNAPS

Draw these photos taken on your holiday!

This is me taking a giant monster for a walk in the blue and purple forest. I had to keep it on its lead or it would have run off and eaten a few people!

This is me playing catch with a pixie called Dolp that I met in the beautiful 'Garden of Binny'. This garden has many strange shaped flowers.

This is me riding a giant purple and green snail in the giants' 'City of Goff'. You can see a giant's foot behind me!

It was a great holiday but I am glad to be home.

PATCHWORK PIXIES

The patchwork pixies have been busy making patterns and sewing squares together to make a pretty quilt. They need your help to finish it. Make up some new patterns and then colour the quilt. They want it to be really colourful.

Free Time Activities 5-7 © Molly Potter

SPOT MIST

A strange spot mist has blown into Flower Wood. Fill in the lines that are hidden by the spot mist to complete the picture. Then colour it in.

MAKE A PATTERN

Draw a neat pattern on each of these items using only the shapes in the box next to it.

Free Time Activities 5-7 © Molly Potter

JALLOP JUNGLE

Read the description below or ask a grown up to read it to you. In Jallop Jungle there are three plants. The Walloo plant has very big, green leaves. It has large, bright red flowers with petals that are this shape (1) and a dark middle that looks like this (2). There is another plant called Trass and it has long, thin, pointy, brown leaves which have blue fruit on the end of them that looks like this (3). The other plant is the Hitty tree which has very lumpy bark with a pattern all over it like this (4). You can often see eyes looking out of the bark like this (5). In Jallop Jungle you will nearly always see a Krattle bird. They love to sit in the Hitty tree. The Krattle bird is purple and blue and has a yellow beak that is this shape (6) and feathers on its head like this (7). The pattern on a Krattle bird's front looks like this (8).

Using the description above and the key on the right, finish the picture of Jallop Jungle.

1
2
3
4
5
6
7
8

Hetty Tree

Thrass

Walloo

PETS NEED HOMES!

Draw a home for each of these pets.

PET: FLOOPTAIL

LIKES
- water
- red plants
- spotty rocks
- mirrors
- swimming through hoops

HATES
- the colour green

PET: NOPSTER

LIKES
- pink straw
- playing with marbles
- ringing bells
- jumping
- triangles

HATES
- the dark

PET: LARROT

LIKES
- sitting on cushions
- to scratch
- circles

HATES
- straight lines

Free Time Activities 5-7 © Molly Potter

ADD TO THIS PICTURE

Ped, Maz, Pif, Rof and Tob are all at the park. They need some colour and pattern added to their picture.

PED   MAZ   PIF   ROF   TOB

WHAT YOU NEED TO DO

- Make 2 things spotty.
- Give one of them a hat.
- Put this pattern on something:

- Colour 2 things red.
- Make something hairy.
- Give one of them two rosy cheeks.
- Give one of them a bag to carry.
- Colour 3 things green.
- Make 2 things stripy.
- Draw some grass at their feet.
- Colour 4 things yellow.
- Colour 1 thing blue.

CRAZY COLOURING

Colour each thing in this picture a colour that it never is! Tree trunks are never blue and the sky is never purple! If something can be any colour (like a plate) then leave it white.

WHO LIVES HERE?

Draw the person, creature, animal or thing you think might live in each of these homes.

WHAT A SPECTACLE!

Rark and Diffy really need you to invent some cool glasses for them. Can you draw them on their faces? Don't forget you need to make sure the glasses are held in place like real people's glasses — either round the ears, on the nose or another way.

RARK

DIFFY

COMPLETE THE CREATURE

Can you complete these pictures so that you end up with a whole creature?

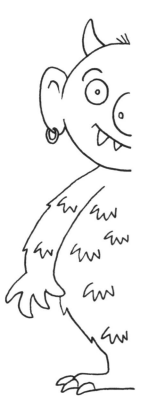

SHAPE ZOO

The animals in this zoo have bodies that are made out of shapes. Draw the animals in their pens and cages. Try to make them look like real animals, even though shape animals don't exist!

RECTANGLE RAFF

CIRCLE CIRPONT

SQUARE SQUILL

STAR STOME

TRIANGLE TRIGOP

Free Time Activities 5-7 © Molly Potter 2008

PHOTO FRAME FRENZY

Here are four people that would like you to design their photo frames.

Colin Colour would like his frame to have as many different colours on it as possible and have absolutely no white on it.

Sarah Swirl would like a blue and green frame with swirls, so that it looks a bit like water.

Maisy Maths would like her frame decorated with red and black numbers in an interesting pattern.

Peter Plant would like his frame decorated with flowers and leaves.

KINGS AND QUEENS

Draw the king and queen of the following two lands. Remember to give them crowns and robes.

The king and queen of the land of *spirals*.

The king and queen of the land of *triangles*.

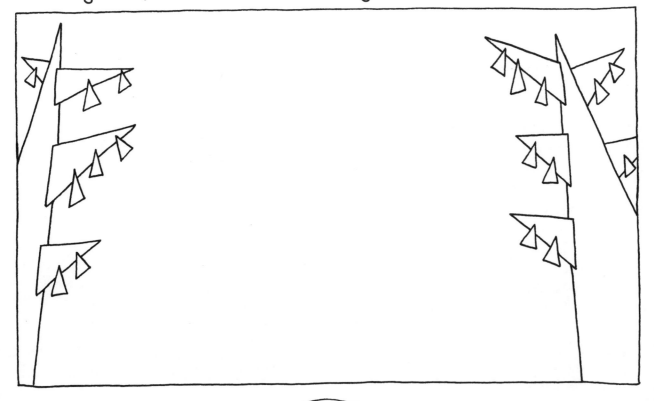

Free Time Activities 5-7 © Molly Potter 2008

CAN YOU FINISH THE PICTURE?

Bobby is a bit forgetful. He started a picture of a girl and a boy but forgot to finish it. Luckily, he did tell his friend what he wanted the picture to be like. Finish the picture for him.

THE GIRL:

- has black curly hair.
- is wearing glasses.
- has blue eyes.
- is looking angry.
- has a dotty pattern on her dress that has at least three colours.
- has stripy tights on.
- is holding an umbrella.
- has red shoes on.

THE BOY:

- has neat brown hair with a fringe.
- has a woolly hat.
- has brown eyes.
- is smiling.
- is wearing a T-shirt with a fish on it.
- has blue shorts.
- is holding a balloon.
- has at least four colours on his socks and big laces on his green shoes.

IN DISGUISE

Use a variety of disguises to make all these faces look different.
Here are some ideas for you to choose from.

Free Time Activities 5-7 © Molly Potter 2008

STORYBOOK COVERS

Can you make up a title and draw a cover for each of these stories?
- A story about the messiest girl in the world
- A story about a perfect child
- A story about a monster school
- A story about aliens having a picnic

Don't forget to give your story an author!

WALLPAPER DESIGN

What wallpaper design do you think each of these four characters might have? Draw your ideas on the wall behind them. Don't forget to colour it.

PETE NEAT

POLLY PATTERN

FLEUR FLOWER

MESSY MONSTER

Free Time Activities 5-7 © Molly Potter 2008

HARD TO FIND

First colour these different places. Then draw the creature that would be hard to see in each place because it is camouflaged so well.

A flower garden

A brick wall

Dotty wallpaper

A rubbish dump

SILLY SUIT

Can you put different patterns and colours on this tie, shirt and
trousers so they look really silly?

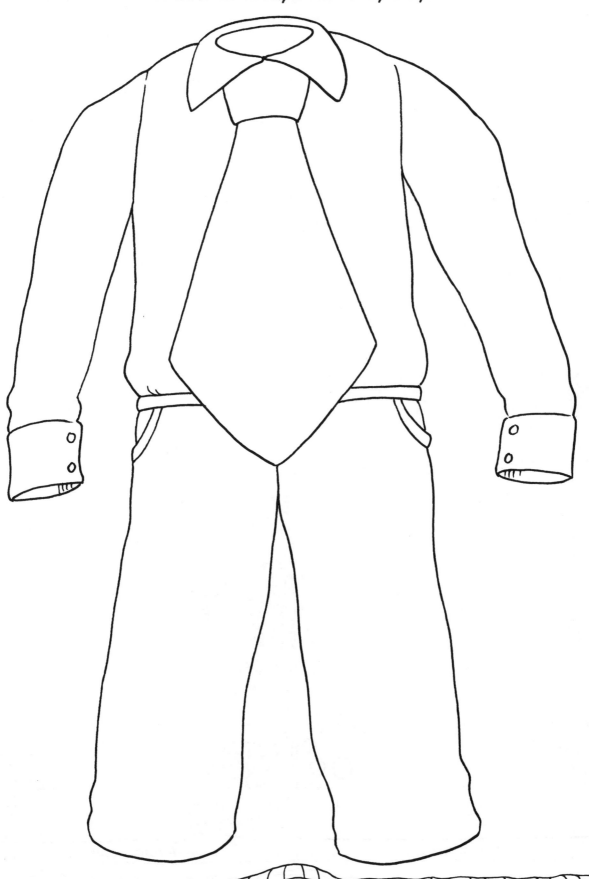

Free Time Activities 5-7 © Molly Potter 2008

TOUCH A LETTER

Try to touch at least one thing that begins with each letter of the alphabet. Write or draw what you touched next to each letter.

a

b

c

d

e

f

g

h

i

j

k

l

m

n

o

p

q

r

s

t

u

v

w

x

y

z

UNDER THE SEA

Add some weird plants and sea creatures to this picture. Try to add at least five fish and two plants. Make them as unusual as you like!

Free Time Activities 5-7 © Molly Potter 2008

DOTS AND CIRCLES

How many black dots and white circles can you find in each picture?
Write the answers on the grid.

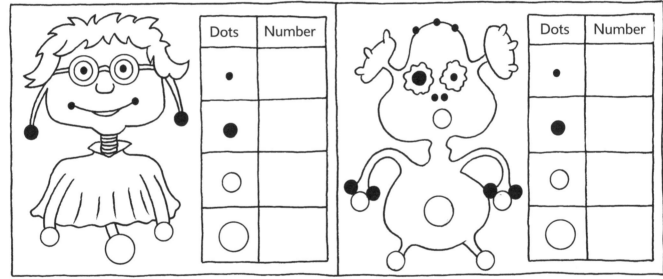

Dots	Number
•	2
●	1
○	5
○	3

MORE TO DO!
Now try and draw two
pictures of your own
with these numbers of
dots and circles.

Dots	Number
•	4
●	2
○	3
○	1

Answer on p64

MIX AND MATCH FACE

On a separate piece of paper draw lots of different faces using these bits!

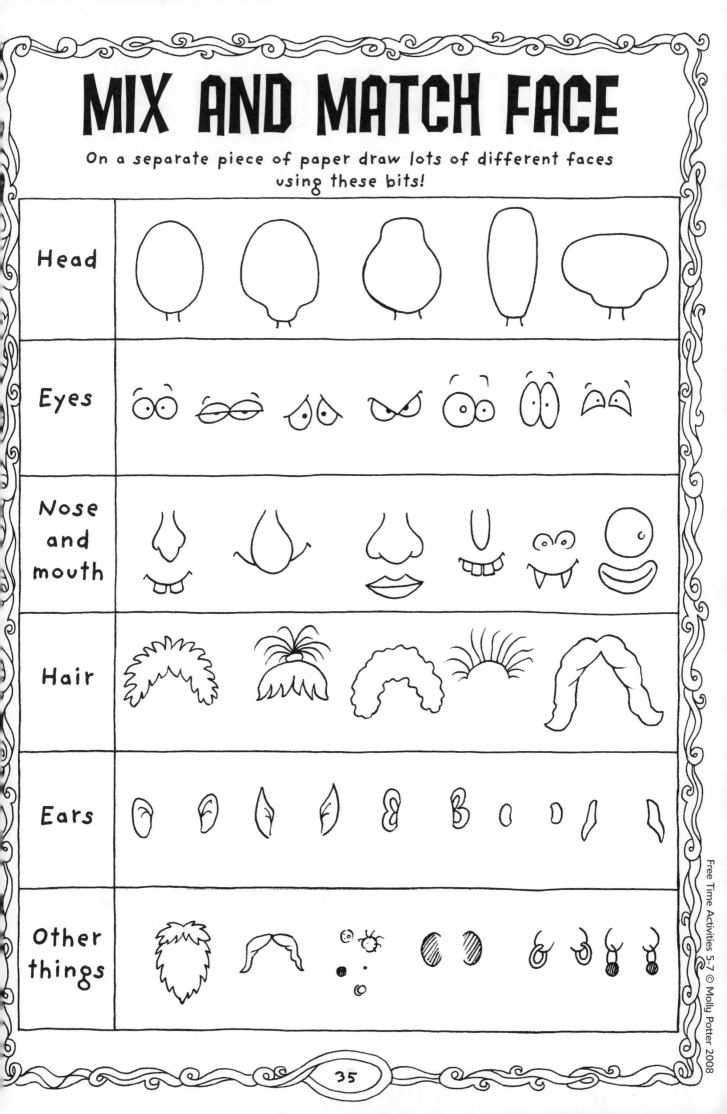

Head	
Eyes	
Nose and mouth	
Hair	
Ears	
Other things	

Free Time Activities 5-7 © Molly Potter 2008

ROBOT ROB

This is Robot Rob playing with his toys.

Colour all the triangles red.

Colour all the squares green.

Colour all the circles blue.

MORE TO DO!
Now have a go at drawing a pet for Robot Rob using only squares, triangle and circles. Give your robot pet a name.

NASTY SPELLS!

A nasty witch has been casting spells. Draw what you think each of these would look like after the spell has been cast.

MORE TO DO!

Now try drawing some creatures of you own, before and after some of these spells have been cast.

• Grows a tail and pointy ears • Has body parts that have disappeared •
• Has smoke coming out of different body parts •
• Gets covered in green and pink spots •
• Grows very large ears, eyes, hands and feet •

Try making up some spells of your own.

Free Time Activities 5–7 © Molly Potter

WHAT-A-MUDDLE-MANDY

Mandy went to Pal Park, came home and drew what she thought she had seen. Mandy often gets things in a muddle. Can you put a ring round the things she has muddled up?

MORE TO DO!
Now have a go at drawing some of these things the way Mandy might draw them!
- A snowman • A face • A car • A rocket • A door • A cat •
- A book • A washing line with washing on it •
- Some tools (saw, hammer, drill, screwdriver) •
- A rowing boat on a lake • Some children playing football •
- A fruit bowl • A television • The sky • A train •

FRUG PARK

Hob and Villy and his pet grarp called Yad went on a trip to Frug Park. They followed the arrows on the map. Hob took his camera. On a separate piece of paper draw four of the photos that Hob took.

FILL UP A STAR

With just one piece of scrap paper and glue (no scissors) can you cover this star without going over the lines or leaving any grey showing?

HAIRDRESSING MAYHEM!

Find lots of different things (e.g. pencil shavings, grass, leaves, twigs, tissue paper) to stick on these heads to give them different hairstyles.

PLANET OB!

In the strange light that comes from the green sun on Planet Ob, you can only see the outline of Zob, Zab and Zib. Draw in the details to show what you think they look like.

MORE TO DO!
Draw the outline of something and ask a friend to draw in the details.

HIDE YOUR NAME

Can you hide all the letters of your name in this pile of messy toys? You need to make it hard to find the letters but not impossible. You can add patterns and lines to the picture to help you hide them. See if a friend can find your hidden letters.

MORE TO DO!
Now try hiding all the letters of the alphabet for your friend to find.

43

DOTTY RACE

Make sure your friend has a copy of this sheet as well.

INSTRUCTIONS
- You and your friend need to start at the same time.
- Join the numbers in order from 1 to 28 with a pencil line.
- Don't touch the black lines at the edges or the dots at all.
(If you do touch them, you have to go back to the beginning.)
- You will need to go quite slowly but remember it's a race!

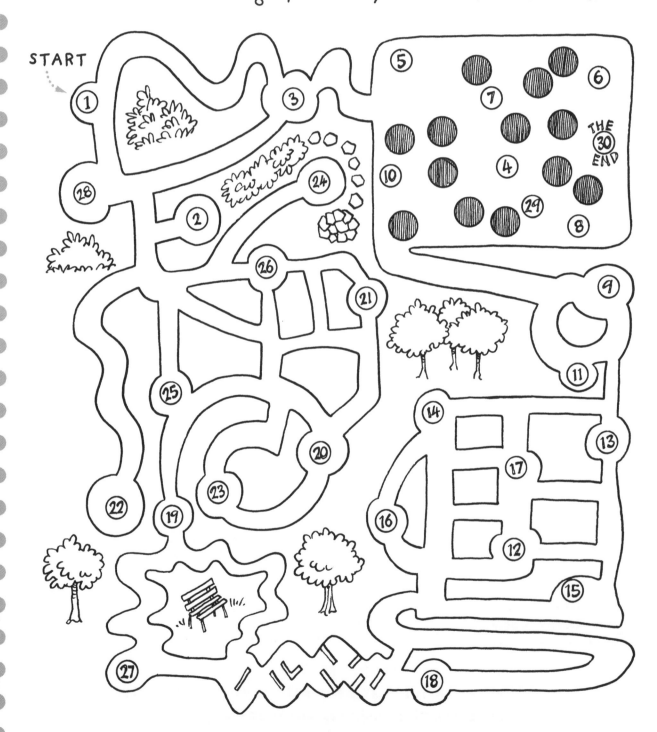

START

THE END 30

PARTY FUSSPOTS

Work with a friend.
You are having a party. Below are all the creatures that are invited to your party. Sadly, they are all very fussy. Each creature has a list of things they love and hate.

From these lists work out:
• what colour the balloons can be • what food to give them •
• what drink to give them • what game to play •

MOOMP

HATES:
pink, music
LOVES:
cake, orange juice

LOP

HATES:
paper, pins, yellow
LOVES:
apple pie, cola

DAFFY

HATES:
hot food
LOVES:
blue, peanut butter sandwiches

MAZ

HATES:
green, sweet food, orange drinks
LOVES:
football, hot dogs, milk

HUPPY

HATES:
blue, sandwiches, donkeys
LOVES:
musical bumps, cheese sandwiches

BOBBIT

HATES:
fruit, wheels, water
LOVES:
peas, skipping, biscuits

MAFOO
HATES:
jumping, fizzy drinks
LOVES:
cold sausage rolls, pin the tail on the donkey, musical statues

TONG

HATES:
chocolate, vegetables, rope
LOVES:
pass the parcel, white, banana, orange squash

PETO

HATES:
games that use a ball
LOVES:
hide and seek, roller skating, lemonade

MORE TO DO!
Draw and name the last person to come to the party.
Luckily, this guest is not fussy at all!

Answer on p64

Free Time Activities 5–7 © Molly Potter 2008

PUT THEM IN ORDER

Put a number next to each thing to show the order.

From smallest to biggest

From lightest to heaviest

From hottest to coldest

From tallest to shortest

From quietest to loudest

From least to most

Number of traffic lights		Legs on a person
	Suns in the sky	
Wheels on a car		Stars in the sky

From lowest to highest

Top of a mountain		Moon
	A beach	Bottom of the sea

NOW LET'S SEE WHAT YOU THINK...

Number these from easiest to hardest

tying shoe laces
learning times tables
juggling
walking

From least scary to most scary

ghosts
spiders
snakes
the dark

From most interesting to most boring

science
playtime
maths
assembly

MORE TO DO!
Make up some lists for other people to put in order.
Use pictures or words.

Answer on p64

HOW MANY?

Work with a partner.
Put the things listed below into one of the boxes.
Put them in:
BOX 1: if they only come on their own.
BOX 2: if they are always a pair.
BOX 3: if they come in threes.
BOX 4: if the come in fours.
The first one has been done for you.

- drumsticks
- traffic lights
- eyes
- legs on a dog
- gloves

- a nose
- blind mice
- twins
- corners of a page

- Goldilocks' bears
- triplets
- socks
- wheels on a bike

- hands on a watch (with a second hand)
- wheels on a car
- corners of a triangle
- ears

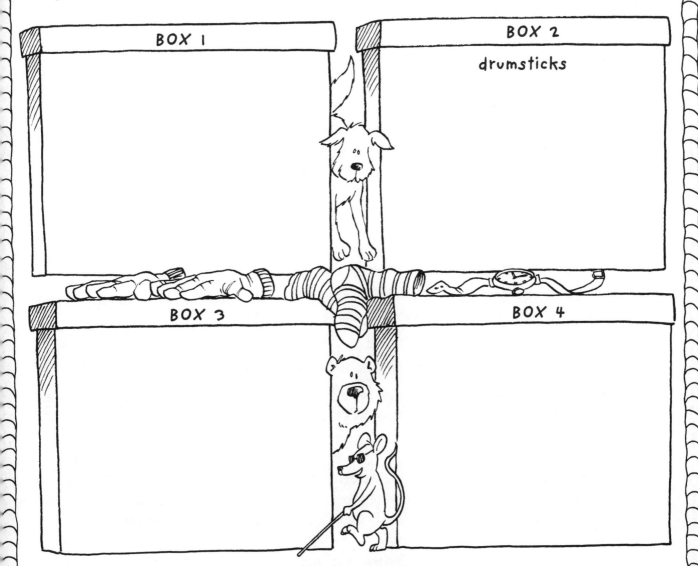

BOX 1	BOX 2
	drumsticks

BOX 3	BOX 4

MORE TO DO!
Can you think of other things to add to each box?

Free Time Activities 5-7 © Molly Potter

TREASURE HUNT

INSTRUCTIONS

1. Work with a partner.
2. Each decide where you are going to hide your treasure and write it down on a piece of paper without your partner seeing.
   (It must be a named place on the map.)
3. You need to try and guess where your partner's treasure is hidden.
4. Take it in turns to guess.
5. Before each guess, you can ask one question that can only be answered by a YES or a NO. You could ask questions like:
   • Is it in a wet place? • Is it in a place that you can go inside?
   • Is it somewhere with a tree or lots of trees?
   • Is it in the north half of the island?
   (Sometimes you might have to say, 'cannot answer' if the answer is not simply a 'yes' or a 'no'.)
6. The first person to guess where his or her partner's treasure is hidden wins that turn.

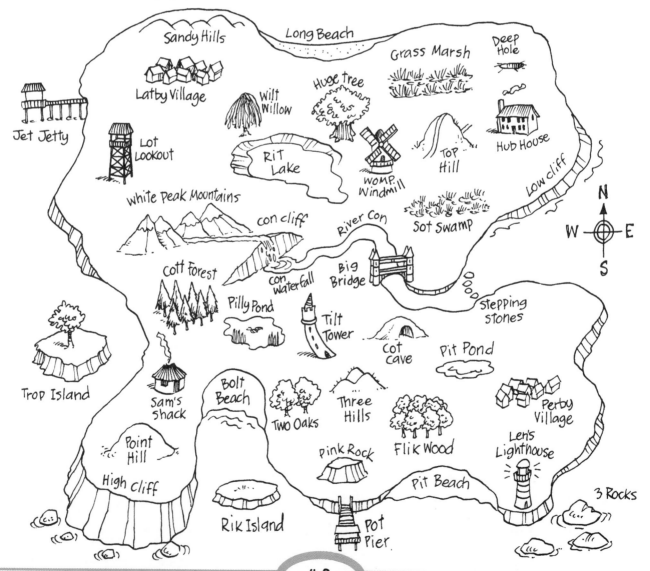

SENSING SOZZ

This is Sozz.

Sozz loves to smell, taste, look at, touch and listen to different things. He has never been to planet earth. He wants you to show him the three best things you think that earth has for him to smell, to taste, to see, to touch and to hear.

Work with a partner and see if you can agree which three things to show to Sozz.

SOZZ COULD	THREE THINGS
smell	
taste	
see	
touch	
hear	

MORE TO DO!
Can you think of the three most horrible things you could put in front of Sozz?

SUPER GOODY, SUPER MISCHIEF-MAKER

This is Gracie. She is as good and well behaved as a person can be! She is always helping other people.

This is Marcie. Marcie would never actually hurt anyone but she is always getting up to mischief. She is extremely naughty.

Gracie and Marcie carry bags full of stuff that helps them to be good or naughty. Here is what can be found in their bags — but the items are all mixed up! Decide who owns each thing and mark it with a G or an M. Make up what either Marcie or Gracie did that was good or naughty, using each thing e.g. the map is Gracie's — she used it to help people who were lost.

glue   teabag   bucket   itching powder

map   ladder   catapult   torch

magnifying glass

apple   marbles   drawing pins

elastic bands   sticky tape   ball of yellow wool

hammer   brown paint

See if you can swap all the things and make up what Marcie and Gracie did with each object.

For example: If Marcie owned the map, she might have used it to find all her friends' houses so she could knock on their doors and then run away!

MADE FROM FOOD!

What would you use to make the following if you could only use food? Talk to a friend about your ideas and then label the pictures with the food you have decided to use.

A snowman

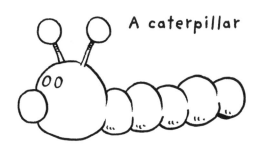

A caterpillar

What sort of food could you use to make a face on this plate? Draw the food face! Don't forget your face needs eyes, a nose, a mouth, ears, hair, cheeks and eyebrows.

Free Time Activities 5-7 © Molly Potter 2008

SHOPPING BAGS

Before you draw anything, discuss your ideas with a friend.
Design a bag for each of these shops. Make sure the shop's name is nice
and clear.

Sid's Smile Shop – where you can
buy a smile that works even if you are sad.

Will's Wish Shop – where you can buy a
wish to give to someone. You could make this
bag look magical with wands and shooting stars.

Wendy's Weather Shop – where
you can buy tomorrow's weather, today.

Pat's Pet Snozzle Shop – where
you can buy Snozzles and everything you
need to look after them. (Snozzles are very
hairy creatures with three short legs).

FILL UP A RAINBOW

Work with a friend. The colours of the rainbow are: red, orange, yellow, green, blue, indigo and violet but for this rainbow we are going to join indigo and violet and call it purple. Try and think of as many things as you can that are always red, or always orange, etc. Draw the things or write the names on this rainbow e.g. green could be frog, grass, peas, or yellow could be sun, bananas, daffodils.

Red | Orange | Yellow | Green | Blue | Purple

STRANGE GREETINGS

When Baroos meet, they bounce the springs on their heads up and down really fast to show that they are happy to see each other.

When Snoogs meet, they touch noses and push them backwards and forwards to say hello.

Snits make sure that their hair gets in a tangle when they greet each other. Then they squeak as loudly as they can.

All of these ways of saying hello to each other make humans look a bit boring.

With a partner, make up as many different ways as you can think of that could be a strange way to greet one another. Try using:

• sounds • feet • knees • hands • your face • ears • elbows • eyes •

MORE TO DO!

Draw two creatures greeting each other in an unusual way like the pictures above.

MIRROR BUDDY

Work with a partner

You are going to try and do the following things so that you both look like there is a mirror between you and one of you is the reflection of the other. You will need to practice this a lot to make it work!

Try doing some of these things:

STILL PICTURES
Stare at something in the distance
- Be at a bus stop looking at your watch
- Be puzzled
- Be a statue of Robin Hood

MOVEMENT
- Hop on one leg
- Look happy then sad then happy again
- Yawn and stretch
- Do some exercises like star jumps and running on the spot
- Move in slow motion
- Dance
- Scratch lots of itches

MIMING
- Brush your teeth
- Eat a really juicy melon
- Walk on a tightrope
- Laugh at something funny
- Cheer on sports day
- Juggle and drop the balls
- Be a melting snowman
- Watch TV, be eating a snack and change the look on your face
- Be a nursery rhyme character

(Miss Muffet, Humpty Dumpty, Little Bo Peep)

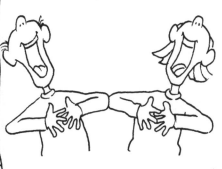

Free Time Activities 5–7 © Molly Potter 2008

SECRET MISSION

NOTES FOR ADULTS

The idea of this activity is to set a secret mission for each child to carry out without being detected. Each mission is different and you need to set it secretly with the individual child. Some tasks need simple equipment and it is best to hand this out with the task, unless it is equipment out in the room already. Make sure that no one does their task before the official start time. Depending on the tasks you set, it might be appropriate to stop children from leaving the room during the time given to complete the mission. A toilet break might be timely before the mission time starts!

Set a time limit for when the mission needs to have been completed. It's a good idea to be doing another quiet activity during the time allocated for completing missions. Tell the children that they need to be observant and spot other people doing their missions as well as completing their own mission.

Once the time limit has been reached, ask the whole group to sit down and tell you about anything they saw that they believe might have been someone completing their mission. If anyone's mission is rumbled, they have failed. You then need to ask each child what their mission was and establish that they actually completed it. If they did not, they too have failed.

POSSIBLE MISSIONS

Write your name on a piece of paper and put it on a wall somewhere.	Use a pencil as a book mark.	Sticky tape a coin to the bottom of a table.	Put an item of clothing on inside out.
Take a sock off and hide it somewhere.	Put a folded piece of paper under a chair leg.	Hook an elastic band somewhere so it is stretched.	Stuff some cotton wool in a corner where it can be seen without having to move anything.
Tie a piece of string around something black or grey.	Pin a small square of coloured material on your clothing somewhere.	Stick a piece of sticky tape on someone else's shoe.	Get another person to clap their hands.

EXAMPLES OF HARDER MISSIONS

Get another person to say the word potato.	Hide something that belongs to someone else in a matchbox and place it on the floor somewhere.	Roll a ball of modelling clay so that it is round, squash it flat and put it in your shoe.
Cut a piece of paper into 6 pieces and hide them in 6 different places.	Draw a circle, colour it red and then cut it out.	Place a chair on its side.

EXAMPLES OF PAIRED MISSIONS

Tie a piece of cotton to two points so it is stretched in a straight line for the length of two tables.	Find something that your partner could use as a ring and put it on their finger.	Swap an item of clothing.

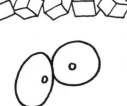
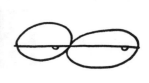

OBSERVATION!

NOTES FOR ADULTS

This activity tests the children's ability to observe and remember details.

1. Scatter a few different objects around an area that will be the 'stage'
e.g. a chair, a scarf, a ball, a skipping rope, a hoop, a few books, a table,
some scrap paper, a pen.

2. Ask one pupil to go on to the 'stage' and do a variety of things (see the
examples below) for a set amount of time. The older the children the longer you
can make the time. For young children, you might need to suggest that the
'performer' moves very slowly and takes only two or three minutes. Demonstrate
some examples of the kind of things they might do:

- sit down, cross his/her legs
- pick up one book, put the book down in a different position
- fold a piece of paper in half
- bounce a ball
- scratch his/her head
- step in and out of the hoop twice
- point to one corner of the table
- cough
- count to three on their fingers
- hop twice
- stare at something
- move the chair
- say something at different points in the 'performance'

3. During the 'performance', make a few notes to remind yourself of questions
you can ask the children – questions that will have required good observation and
memory skills to answer e.g.

- What did s/he do just before sat down?
- Where was the book before it was moved?
- Which way did s/he fold the paper?
- How many times did s/he bounce the ball?
- Which part of her/his body did s/he scratch?
- How many times did s/he step inside the hoop?
- What did s/he point at?

4. As you ask the questions, choose the first child who indicates they might know
the answer (usually by putting their hand up) to give their answer. The child that
gets the most questions right becomes the next 'performer'.

5. As the children get better at observation, make the 'performances' longer and
include more objects.

Free Time Activities 5-7 © Molly Potter 2008

THE RIGHT ROUTE

The aim of this activity is to be the person who finally works out how to get from the start to the finish by working out the one 'allowed' way of doing this.

Lay out a small number of objects (2 or 3) on the floor, for example:

skipping rope

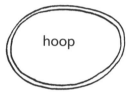
hoop

beanbag

Before playing this game with the children, you need to decide a way of travelling over, under, through, around etc these objects so that this becomes the only 'allowed' way of travelling from the start to the finish. You need to make a clear mental note of this. Here are a few suggested routes:

ROUTE 1

With the selected equipment above, children might need to travel along the rope with their legs straddling either side of it, then walk twice around the hoop and then put the beanbag on their head and then back on the floor.

ROUTE 2

They need to pick up the rope and skip with it once, put it back down in a straight line, then jump in the hoop and raise it up over their head and place it on the floor so they are no longer inside it and then kick the bean bag ahead of them.

Tell the children that there is only one 'allowed' way of getting from the start to the finish and give some examples of what you might need to do at each object to demonstrate this. Through trial and error they have to try and work out which is the 'allowed' way of travelling.

Ask the children to line up at the start in a way that enables them to see all the equipment. Then ask the children to attempt travelling from the start to the finish, one at a time. The moment their attempt does not include the allowed route, you need to say 'stop' and send the child to the back of the line so the next child in line can start their attempt. If the children struggle, you can give clues by saying 'cold', 'warm', 'getting warmer' etc after each child's attempt. The winner is the person who works out the allowed route and makes it through to the end.

Once the children have got the idea of the game, they can make up their own allowed routes (with some adult guidance to prevent it from becoming too obscure) for other children to try and work out.

BE THE FIRST TO BRING ME...

NOTES FOR ADULTS

This simple game is about children being the first to present you with what you read out. You need to stress that the thing needs to be in their hand when they present it.

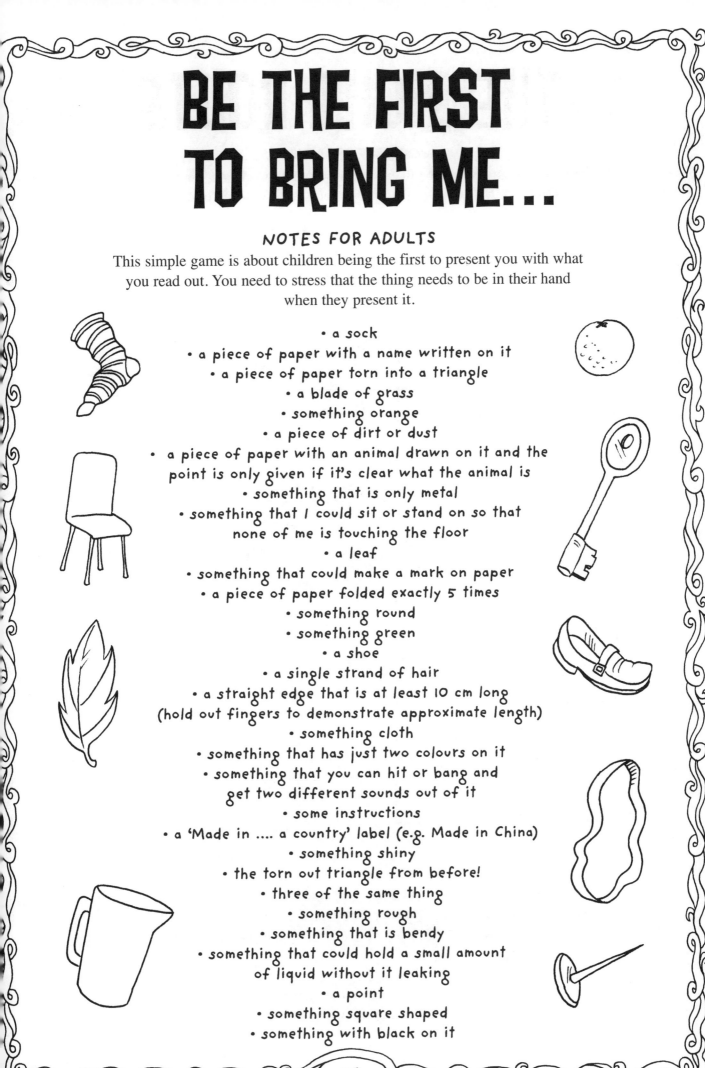

- a sock
- a piece of paper with a name written on it
- a piece of paper torn into a triangle
- a blade of grass
- something orange
- a piece of dirt or dust
- a piece of paper with an animal drawn on it and the point is only given if it's clear what the animal is
- something that is only metal
- something that I could sit or stand on so that none of me is touching the floor
- a leaf
- something that could make a mark on paper
- a piece of paper folded exactly 5 times
- something round
- something green
- a shoe
- a single strand of hair
- a straight edge that is at least 10 cm long (hold out fingers to demonstrate approximate length)
- something cloth
- something that has just two colours on it
- something that you can hit or bang and get two different sounds out of it
- some instructions
- a 'Made in .... a country' label (e.g. Made in China)
- something shiny
- the torn out triangle from before!
- three of the same thing
- something rough
- something that is bendy
- something that could hold a small amount of liquid without it leaking
- a point
- something square shaped
- something with black on it

Free Time Activities 5–7 © Molly Potter 2008

WHERE'S IT FROM?

This activity needs preparation. You need to draw 'rectangles' that show snippets of a scene from the place that you are in e.g. you might draw something like this:

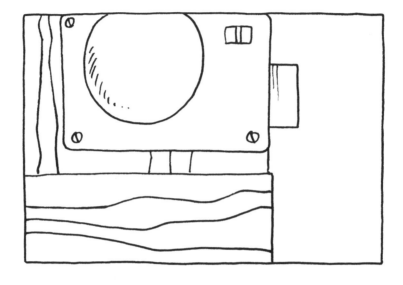

OR

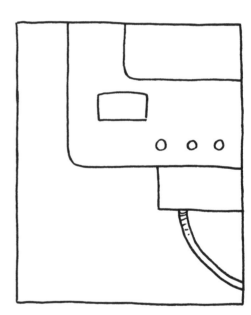

The children then need to 'hunt' for the images that you drew and either make a mental note, or indicate where the picture is from on a simple map. Children could then have a go at drawing some of their own rectangles for other people to find.

This activity, can of course, be prepared using photos from a digital camera – if one is available.

BODY PARTS!

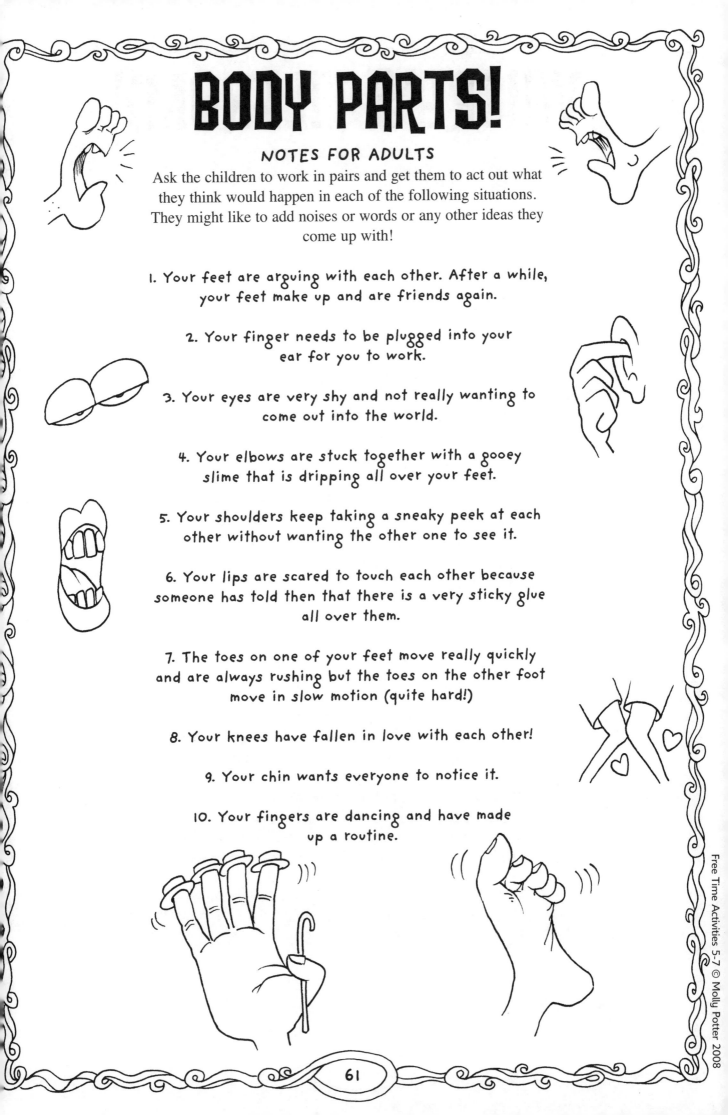

NOTES FOR ADULTS

Ask the children to work in pairs and get them to act out what they think would happen in each of the following situations. They might like to add noises or words or any other ideas they come up with!

1. Your feet are arguing with each other. After a while, your feet make up and are friends again.

2. Your finger needs to be plugged into your ear for you to work.

3. Your eyes are very shy and not really wanting to come out into the world.

4. Your elbows are stuck together with a gooey slime that is dripping all over your feet.

5. Your shoulders keep taking a sneaky peek at each other without wanting the other one to see it.

6. Your lips are scared to touch each other because someone has told then that there is a very sticky glue all over them.

7. The toes on one of your feet move really quickly and are always rushing but the toes on the other foot move in slow motion (quite hard!)

8. Your knees have fallen in love with each other!

9. Your chin wants everyone to notice it.

10. Your fingers are dancing and have made up a routine.

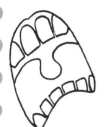

VOICE CHALLENGES!

NOTES FOR ADULTS
Introduce these challenges one at a time.

1. Who in the group can use their voice to make the highest
note and the deepest note?

2. Ask everyone in the group to cover their eyes with blindfolds or ask them
not to look. Shuffle the group around so that no one stays in the same place. Choose
one person by tapping them on the shoulder and tell them to disguise their voice so
that no one can guess who they are. Get them to say:
"Bet you can't guess who I am."

3. Organize the children into pairs and ask them to make up a funny sound that could
be two aliens talking together. Suggest that both aliens speak the same language, so
they should both sound similar. Then ask them to have a conversation about the
weather including gestures!

4. Put children into pairs. Tell the children that they have lost their voices. See if each
pair can guess what their partner is telling them by lip reading alone. Suggest that
each child tells their partner about something they have done today.

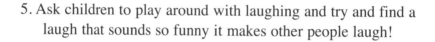

5. Ask children to play around with laughing and try and find a
laugh that sounds so funny it makes other people laugh!

6. Ask the children to make up a sound for the
following imaginary creatures:
* Snub-nosed Troffle
* a Tak Tak bird
* a Long-legged Scralk
Ask the children to practise the sounds for each creature so
that they are the same each time they do them.

7. Ask children to try and make up some of the following:
* the voice of Humpty Dumpty before and after he fell off the wall
* the voice of a bee, if it could speak, telling a flower off
* a ghost singing 'Baa baa black sheep' or another song
* a robot trying to make friends with a kettle
* the voice of a fish complaining that the water it is
swimming in is too muddy

Free Time Activities 5–7 © Molly Potter 2008

ANSWERS

MUDDLE HEADS (P6)

LETTER HUNT (P7)
The word is: HELLO

SPOT WHAT'S THE SAME (P8)

- One curly strand of hair
- The eyes
- The eyebrows
- The earring
- One shoe shape
- One shoelace
- The flower petals
- The spot on the nose
- The belt buckle
- One tooth
- The ears
- Both hand shapes
- The lightening logo on the tie/pocket
- The leaf on the stalk of the flower

CHOSEN NAME (P9)

Prush	Karinta	Soomp
Toplix	Punnip	Fanaf
Tilempapa	Flinta	Solly

DOTS AND CIRCLES (P34)

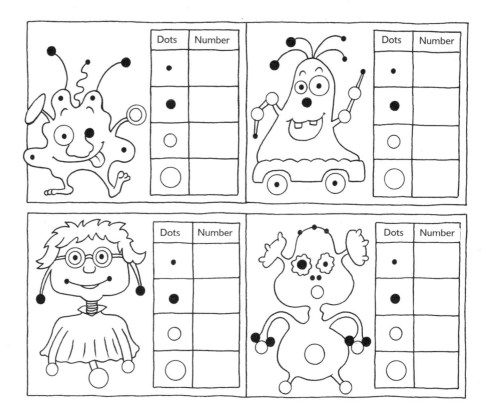

PARTY FUSSPOTS (P45)
Answer: white balloons, cold sausage rolls, milk, hide and seek.

PUT THEM IN ORDER (P64)

FROM SMALLEST TO BIGGEST
- Pin
- Matchbox
- Brick
- Computer
- Car

FROM HOTTEST TO COLDEST
- Boiling water
- Melted chocolate
- A puddle
- Ice

FROM QUIETEST TO LOUDEST
- Silence
- Whisper
- Talk
- Shout

FROM LOWEST TO HIGHEST
- Bottom of the sea
- A beach
- Top of a mountain
- moon

FROM LIGHTEST TO HEAVIEST
- A crisp
- A shoe
- A table
- A lorry

FROM TALLEST TO SHORTEST
- Giraffe
- Elephant
- Dog
- Mouse

FROM LEAST TO MOST
- Suns in the sky
- Legs on a person
- Number of traffic lights
- Wheels on a car
- Stars in the sky